# The Commerson's Dolphin Story

# The Commerson's Dolphin Story

PART OF THE SEAWORLD EDUCATION SERIES

**Research/Writing/Layout**
Deborah Nuzzolo

**Technical Advisors**
Brad Andrews
Dr. Ann E. Bowles
Steve Clark
Dave Force
Tom Goff
James McBain, D.V.M.
Michael Scarpuzzi
Mike Shaw
Glenn Young

**Education Directors**
Hollis J. Gillespie
John Lowe
Ann Quinn
Sheila Voss
Joy L. Wolf

**Editorial Staff**
Judith Coats
Catherine Gregos
Danielle Magee
Deborah Nuzzolo
Donna Parham
Patti Schick
Loran Wlodarski

**Illustrations**
August Stein

**Photos**
Mike Aguilera
SeaWorld San Diego Adventure Camp
SeaWorld San Diego Photo Department

**Photographs**

**Cover:** This book explores the Commerson's Dolphin *(Cephalorhynchus commersonii)*.

**Title page:** The Commerson's dolphin is sometimes called the piebald dolphin. "Piebald" means spotted or patched with black and white.

Published by the SeaWorld Education Department
500 Sea World Drive, San Diego, California, 92109-7904

ISBN 1-893698-10-6
Printed in the United States of America.

T31079

# Contents

# Commerson's Characteristics

The Commerson's
dolphin is named
for French botanist,
naturalist, and
explorer Philibert
Commerson, who
noted them on his
travels to South
America in 1767.

**Despite the distance between populations, most scientists currently recognize only one Commerson's dolphin species.**

# The Piebald Dolphin

How would you recognize a Commerson's dolphin if you saw one? This dolphin's black and white color pattern is its most unique characteristic. In fact, the Commerson's dolphin is sometimes called the *piebald* dolphin. "Piebald" means spotted or patched with black and white.

With a full grown length of just 1.5 m (5 ft.), it's hard to believe that this dolphin is in the same family as another black and white dolphin, the 6.7-m (22-ft.) killer whale (*Orcinus orca*). But it is!

Dolphins, porpoises, and whales belong to the scientific order Cetacea. Cetacea is derived from the Greek word for "a whale." Cetaceans are further divided into three suborders: Odontoceti (toothed whales), Mysticeti (baleen whales), and Archaeoceti (extinct whales of which only fossils remain). Scientists group most dolphins (about 30 species) in the scientific family Delphinidae, part of the suborder Odontoceti.

Delphinids include not only Commerson's dolphins, but also such well known species as bottlenose dolphins, common dolphins, and killer whales. The Commerson's dolphin belongs to the genus *Cephalorhynchus*, which includes three other dolphin species—Heaviside's, Hector's, and Black (Chilean) dolphins. This book discusses the Commerson's dolphin, *Cephalorhynchus commersonii*.

killer whale and calf

The Commerson's dolphin (right) is in the same family as the killer whale (above). Though both dolphins are black and white, their color patterns differ significantly.

Commerson's dolphin

# Philibert Commerson (1727-73)

Philibert Commerson was a French naturalist, botanist, and explorer who sailed on an around-the-world expedition with Louis Antoine de Bougainville in 1766. In 1767 the explorers reached southern South America. It was here that Philibert Commerson noted the small black and white dolphin, which was named "Commerson's dolphin" in his honor.

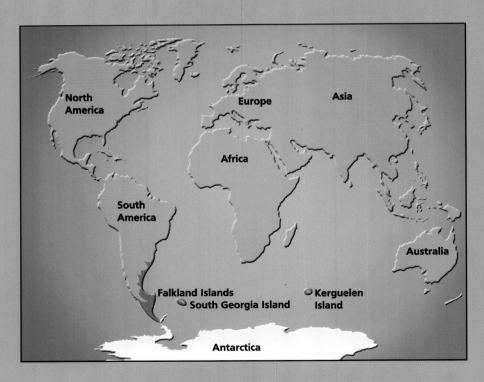

Commerson's dolphins live along the coasts of southern South America, as well as around the Falkland Islands, South Georgia Island, and Kerguelen Island.

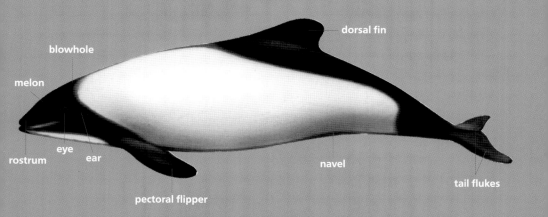

blowhole

dorsal fin

melon

rostrum

eye

ear

pectoral flipper

navel

tail flukes

The Commerson's dolphin, like other whales, has forelimbs modified into flippers, a horizontally flattened tail, a nostril at the top of the head for breathing, and no hind limbs. The dolphin's streamlined shape glides easily through water.

# Commerson's dolphin quick facts

*adult length:* 120 to 170 cm (3.9–5.6 ft.)

*adult weight:* 35 to 60 kg (77–132 lb.)

*length at birth:* 55 to 65 cm (21.7–25.6 in.)

*weight at birth:* 4.5 to 7.3 kg (10–16 lb.)

*food:* krill, cuttlefish, squid, shrimp, and small fishes

*food intake:* about 3.5 to 6 kg (8–13 lb.) each day

*predators:* possibly killer whales and sharks

*swimming speed:* 11 to 13 kph (7–8 mph)

*longevity:* 15 to 18 years

## Distribution and Habitat

Take a look at the red highlighted areas of the map on page 4. You'll see that Commerson's dolphins live along the coasts of southern South America, the Falkland Islands, and South Georgia Island. These dolphins also live in shallow coastal waters around Kerguelen Island in the southern Indian Ocean.

If you have a world atlas, you can take an even closer look at Commerson dolphin distribution. On the west coast of South America in the Pacific Ocean, Commerson's are found as far north as Isla Grande De Chloé, Chile (42°45'S latitude). On the east coast of

Commerson's dolphins live in cold, inshore waters along coastlines, bays, harbors, and river mouths.

South America in the Atlantic Ocean, Commerson's dolphins are found as far north as southern Brazil at about 31°S latitude. The dolphin's distribution extends as far south as the South Shetland Islands, about 63°S latitude.

Commerson's dolphins are also frequently seen in the Strait of Magellan and around Tierra del Fuego, both about 54°S latitude. The Strait of Magellan is a narrow strip of water that connects the Pacific and Atlantic oceans. It also separates Tierra del Fuego, a 241-km (150-mile) peninsula, from mainland South America.

The Commerson's black and white color pattern, a type of camouflage called disruptive coloration, may help conceal the small dolphin from predators or prey.

## *Habitat.*

Commerson's dolphins live in cold, inshore waters along coastlines, bays, harbors, and river mouths. They prefer waters less than 200 m (656 ft.) deep. The water temperature around their South America habitat ranges from 4°C to 16°C (39.2°F–60.8°F). The water temperatures around Kerguelen Island are even colder, 1°C to 8°C (33.8°F–46.4°F).

## Population and Status

The worldwide population of Commerson's dolphins is unknown. Most dolphins sighted are near areas of greatest human activity or in areas like the Strait of Magellan where dolphin observation programs are underway.

Since the Commerson's dolphin distribution is outside of the United States, U.S. Fish and Wildlife Service does not list this dolphin as either threatened or endangered. However, Commerson's dolphins are protected in the South American countries of Argentina (since 1974) and Chile (since 1977).

The international organization, IUCN — The World Conservation Union, lists the Commerson's dolphin in their *2003 IUCN Red List of Threatened Species* in the "Data Deficient" category. This means that there is not enough information about the Commerson's dolphin population to assess the dolphin's risk of extinction. However, because Commerson's dolphins live close to the shore, they are susceptible to accidental netting or entanglement in fishing gear used in coastal areas.

Convention on International Trade in Endangered Species of Wild Fauna and Flora (CITES) is an international treaty that regulates trade in certain wildlife species. All toothed whales, including Commerson's dolphins, are listed on CITES Appendix II. Appendix II includes species identified as threatened, or likely to become endangered if trade isn't regulated.

**The average lifespan for a Commerson's dolphin is 15 to 18 years. Some Commerson's dolphins at SeaWorld are more than 20 years old.**

Commerson's dolphin characteristics include its striking black and white coloration, stocky body, and rounded dorsal fin. Its rostrum resembles those of porpoises—short and blunt rather than long and beaklike like most dolphins.

Despite the distance between South American and Kerguelen Commerson's dolphin populations, most scientists currently recognize only one Commerson's dolphin species. When scientists compared the dolphins in Kerguelen waters with those around South America, they noticed certain differences in their physical features. Kerguelen dolphins are larger than those close to South America. Also, Kerguelen dolphins are black, white, and gray—not just black and white like the dolphins of South America.

The Commerson's black and white color pattern is a type of camouflage called disruptive coloration. This color pattern contradicts the dolphin's body shape,

The male dolphin (left) has an oval patch on its underside. The female's (right) patch is V-shaped.

**Commerson's dolphins average 120 to 170 cm (3.9–5.6 ft.) in length.**

and may help conceal the small dolphin from prey or predators. The Commerson's dolphin's color pattern also gives us a way to visually distinguish males and females. The male dolphin has a large teardrop or heart-shaped black patch on its white underside, while the female has a small oval, arrowhead or V-shaped black patch on her white underside.

*Size.*

Throughout their distribution, dolphins average 120 to 170 cm (3.9–5.6 ft.) and weigh 35 to 60 kg (77–132 lb.). In South American waters, the maximum length of males is about 145 cm (4.75 ft.) while females are 147 to 152 cm (4.8–5 ft.). The larger Kerguelen dolphin males may measure as much as 168 cm (5.5 ft.) long and females as much as 175 cm (5.75 ft.). Mature females tend to grow slightly larger than males.

The Commerson's dolphin's rostrum resembles those of porpoises—short and blunt rather than long and beaklike like most dolphins.

# Head Highlights

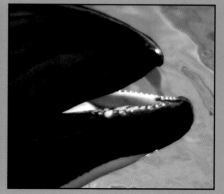

A dolphin's eyes are on the sides of the head, near the corners of the mouth. Dolphins have good vision both in and out of the water. A dolphin's eye is particularly adapted for seeing under water.

Inside a Commerson's dolphin's mouth, small pointed teeth are adapted for grasping, not chewing, food. Most individuals have 26 to 35 teeth on each side of both jaws, a total of 104 to 140 teeth.

Ears, located just behind the eyes, are small inconspicuous openings, with no external ear flaps. Dolphins have a well developed, keen sense of hearing.

A dolphin's rounded dorsal fin and flattened flukes contain no bone, cartilage, or muscle.

### *Fins, Flippers, and Flukes.*

The dolphin's tapered, fusiform body, together with its flippers, flukes, and dorsal fin, adapt this mammal for ocean life. A dolphin's forelimbs are pectoral flippers. Pectoral flippers have the major skeletal elements of land mammal forelimbs, but are fore-shortened and modified. As it swims, a dolphin uses its pectoral flippers to steer and, with the help of the flukes, to stop. The Commerson's dolphin's flippers have rounded tips.

Each lobe of a dolphin's tail is called a fluke. Flukes are flattened pads of tough, dense, fibrous connective tissue, completely without bone, cartilage, or muscle. A dolphin uses the powerful muscles along its back and tail stalk to move the flukes up and down. This motion propels the dolphin forward through water.

Like the flukes, the Commerson's rounded dorsal fin has no bone, cartilage, or muscle inside. The dorsal fin may act as both a heat exchange mechanism and as a keel—it may provide additional resistance when the dolphin turns. The fin is not essential for balance.

## Blowhole.

A Commerson's dolphin breathes through a single blowhole located on the top of its head. The blowhole is covered by a muscular flap, which provides a watertight seal. When the blowhole is closed, the muscle is relaxed. To open the blowhole, a dolphin contracts the muscle.

A dolphin holds its breath while below water. It opens its blowhole and begins to exhale just before reaching the surface of the water. At the surface, the dolphin quickly inhales and then relaxes the muscular flap to close its blowhole.

As a dolphin exhales, seawater that has collected around the blowhole is carried up with the respiratory gases. Seawater and the water vapor condensing in the respiratory gases as they expand in the cooler air form the visible blow of a dolphin.

**To open its blowhole, a dolphin contracts the muscular flap that covers it.**

How do Commerson's dolphins stay warm in such cold water? As a family, dolphins have several thermoregulatory strategies to help them maintain their core temperature, including body shape, blubber, and countercurrent heat exchange.

*Body shape.* Their fusiform body shape and reduced limb size decrease the amount of surface area exposed to the external environment. This helps dolphins conserve body heat.

*Blubber.* Lying just underneath a dolphin's skin is a thick blubber layer. Dolphins deposit most of their body fat here. Blubber insulates the dolphin and streamlines the body. Like other fat, blubber also functions as an energy reserve.

*Countercurrent heat exchange.* A dolphin's circulatory system adjusts to conserve or dissipate body heat and maintain body temperature. Veins surround

**Countercurrent heat exchange aids dolphins in conserving body heat.**

**Lying just underneath a dolphin's skin is a thick blubber layer**

arteries in the flippers, flukes, and dorsal fin. Thus, some heat from the blood traveling through the arteries is transferred to the venous blood rather than the environment. This countercurrent heat exchange aids dolphins in conserving body heat.

Additionally, when a dolphin dives, blood is shunted away from the surface of the body. This decrease in circulation also conserves body heat.

During prolonged exercise or in warm water, a dolphin may need to shed excess heat. In this case, circulation increases to blood vessels near the surface of the flippers, flukes, and dorsal fin, and decreases to blood vessels circulating blood to the body core.

# Commerson's Conduct

Commerson's dolphins are quick and active animals. Leaping, spinning, and surfing are common behaviors.

**Commerson's dolphins are typically found alone or in small groups of 2 to 3 individuals.**

## Social Behavior

Commerson's dolphins are typically found alone or in small groups of two to three individuals. Other observers report groups of 2 to 15, 20 to 30, and on rare occasion, groups of 100 or more Commerson's dolphins swimming together.

Little is known about Commerson's dolphin movements from one area to another. Seasonal movements may be in response to food availability.

These active predators eat a wide variety of food from both open water and the sea floor. They consume many types of small fishes, as well as invertebrates such as krill, squid, cuttlefish, crab, and shrimp.

Dolphins do not chew their food. Usually they swallow fish whole. Commerson's dolphins have high energy needs, and adults eat about 10% of their body weight in food daily. For comparison, an adult bottlenose dolphin eats approximately 4% to 5% of its body weight in food daily.

Commerson's dolphins eat a variety of foods such as smelt and other small fishes.

**Commerson's dolphins commonly swim upside down.**

# Swimming and Diving

Commerson's dolphins are fast and highly maneuverable dolphins. They leap; spin; ride waves, swells, and breaking surf; and swim beside ships. They routinely swim at moderate speeds of about 11 to 13 kph (7–8 mph) and stay below water for 15 to 20 seconds at a depth of about 1 to 1.5 m (3–5 ft.).

Commerson's dolphins often swim upside down and feed in this position as well. Swimming upside down may give the dolphins the advantage of spotting prey swimming above them.

All marine mammals have special physiological adaptations for diving. These adaptations enable a dolphin to conserve oxygen. For example, dolphins, like other marine mammals, have a slower heart rate while diving. When diving, blood is shunted away from tissues tolerant of low oxygen levels toward the heart, lungs, and brain, where oxygen is needed.

Additionally, a dolphin's muscle has a high content of the oxygen-binding protein myoglobin. Myoglobin stores oxygen and helps prevent muscle oxygen deficiency.

Dolphins rely heavily on sound production and reception to navigate, communicate, and hunt in dark or murky waters. Under these conditions, sight is of little use.

Studies suggest that the most likely site of sound production is a tissue complex in the nasal region. Movements of air in the trachea and nasal sacs probably produce sounds. Technological advances in bioacoustic research enable scientists to better explore a dolphin's nasal region.

Commerson's dolphins likely rely as much on sound as they do on sight to hunt prey in the choppy, murky waters of their habitat.

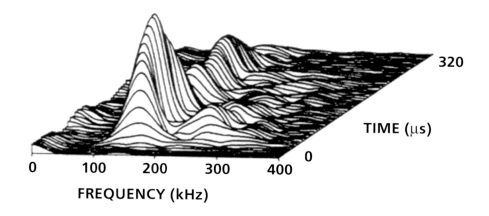

**320**

**TIME (μs)**

**0**

| 0 | 100 | 200 | 300 | 400 |

**FREQUENCY (kHz)**

This diagram shows the amplitude waveform of a single pulse emitted by a Commerson's dolphin. In general, a pulse is 125 to 135 kHz. The symbol μs represents microsecond.

Acoustic recordings of Commerson's dolphins by Hubbs–SeaWorld Research Institute scientists have provided insight. Although Commerson's dolphin sounds are mostly inaudible to us, the dolphins vocalize continually, producing high-frequency, narrow-band pulses of 125 to 135 kHz. Not only is this range beyond human hearing, but it's also above the frequency range for other dolphin species like the bottlenose. Commerson's dolphin vocalizations must be slowed down at least eight times for most people to hear them.

### Echolocation.

Dolphins depend on sound at least as much as sight for a "picture" of their surroundings. This process is called *echolocation*. Dolphins locate and discriminate objects by projecting high-frequency sound waves and listening for echoes. Commerson's dolphins echolocate by producing sound pulses and then receiving and interpreting the resulting echo.

Commerson's use echolocation to find food near the seafloor.

Pulses pass through the melon (rounded region of a dolphin's forehead), which consists of lipids (fats). The melon acts as an acoustical lens to focus these sound waves into a beam, which is projected forward into water in front of the animal.

Sound waves travel through water at a speed of about 1.5 km/sec (0.9 mi./sec.), which is 4.5 times faster than sound traveling through air. These sound waves bounce off objects in the water and return to the dolphin in the form of an echo. The major areas of sound reception are the fat-filled cavities of the lower jawbones. The lower jawbones receive and conduct sounds through the lower jaw to the middle ear, inner ear, and then to hearing centers in the brain via the auditory nerve. The brain receives the sound waves in the form of nerve impulses, which relay the messages of sound and enable the dolphin to interpret the sound's meaning.

Most dolphins that are confirmed echolocators, like the bottlenose dolphin, use broadband clicks for their echolocation. The acoustic energy in these brief clicks (about 50 to 128 microseconds) is spread over a wide band of frequencies including the lower part of the human hearing range. However, Commerson's dolphins produce directional, narrow band pulses. Each pulse lasts about 100 to 1,200 microseconds. The acoustic energy in these longer pulses is in a narrow band of frequencies very near the top of the known dolphin hearing range.

By this complex system of echolocation, dolphins can determine size, shape, speed, distance, direction, and even some of the internal structure of objects in the water. They are able to learn and later recognize the echo signatures returned by preferred prey species. The high frequency pulses of Commerson's dolphins are good for "seeing" fine details of objects on the seafloor. This correlates with the coastal seafloor food preferences of these dolphins.

**Commerson's vocalizations must be slowed down at least 8 times for most people to hear them.**

Many details of echolocation are not completely understood. Studies by scientists at the Hubbs-SeaWorld Research Institute and elsewhere have shown details about bioacoustics not otherwise available. Research on echolocation continues.

## Longevity

A Commerson's dolphin's typical life span is 15 to 18 years. Some Commerson's dolphins at SeaWorld are more than 20 years old.

### Causes of death.

Natural predators may include killer whales, sharks, and leopard seals because they live in the same areas as Commerson's dolphins. However there are no documented observations of predation.

As in any animal population, a variety of diseases and parasites also can be responsible for dolphin deaths. Dolphins may suffer from viral, bacterial, and fungal infections. Parasites that may affect dolphins include roundworms and flukes.

### Human impact.

Because Commerson's dolphins live close to shore, they are susceptible to accidental netting or entanglement in fishing gear used in coastal areas. Commerson's dolphins have also been illegally hunted in Chile and Argentina waters for use as bait in the southern king crab fishery.

Yet even when they're not hunted these coastal dolphins may be affected by habitat destruction and pollution.

Coastal dolphins, Commerson's are susceptible to accidental entanglement in fishing gear.

*Commerson's Calf*

On February 22,
1985 a Commerson's
calf was born at
SeaWorld San Diego.
Several more births
have occurred since,
giving scientists
firsthand knowledge
about these baby
dolphins.

Births take place during the early spring through late summer of the Southern Hemisphere, October through March. Calves are born in the water, tail-first. A newborn Commerson's dolphin is about 55 to 65 cm (21.7– 25.6 in.) in length and weighs 4.5 to 7.3 kg (10–16 lb). This heavy calf makes up about 22% of the mother's body weight and is about 61% her length. In comparison, a bottlenose dolphin calf composes only about 10% of the mother's weight and is about 46% her length.

A Commerson's dolphin calf is gray at birth. Its skin shows several vertical creases, a result of fetal folding. These folds disappear in about a week. Additionally, the dolphin calf's dorsal fin and tail flukes are pliable and lack firmness, but gradually stiffen.

**A Commerson's calf and its mother swim together.**

**A newborn Commerson's dolphin has gray skin and birth folds.**

### Nursing

Nursing begins shortly after birth. A calf nurses
under water, close to the surface. The calf suckles
from nipples concealed in abdominal mammary
slits. The mother's rich milk helps the baby rapidly
develop a thick blubber layer.

### Growth

Calves grow quickly. One-year-old calves are about
99 to 117 cm. (39–46 in.). Compare this to the average
adult length of 120 to 170 cm (47–67 in.) and you'll
see that a large one-year-old can be virtually the same
size as a small adult.

# Commerson's Dolphin Baby Book

A dolphin calf is usually born tail-first in the water.

Mom helps the calf to the surface for its first breath.

The calf's floppy flukes will stiffen as the calf explores its surroundings. Fins and flukes contain fibrous connective tissue, not bones.

The dolphin calf nurses from its mom. Fat-rich milk helps the calf develop an insulating blubber layer beneath its skin.

A Commerson's dolphin calf is dark gray at birth.

As it grows, the calf becomes black and white like its mom.

## Gestation and Maturity

Gestation is about 12 months. South American and Kerguelen Commerson's differ from one another in ages and lengths of sexual maturity. A female from the South American population is sexually mature and can bear a calf when she is 5 to 8 years old and about 130 cm (51 in.). Males are mature at about 5 to 6 years old and 127 to 131 cm (50–51.6 in.). A female from the Kerguelen population is sexually mature when she is about 5 years old and 165 cm (65 in.). Males are mature at about 8 years old.

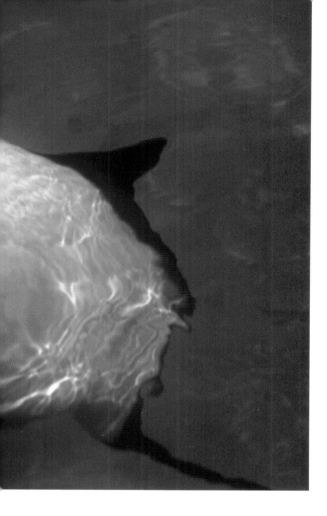

A Commerson's dolphin calf grows quickly. In the first year of birth a calf grows about 36 to 47 cm (14–18.5 in.).

## Historical Birth

The first Commerson's dolphin born in a marine zoological park was born at SeaWorld San Diego on February 22, 1985. This and subsequent calves have provided a wealth of information about the species in general and about growth and nutritional requirements specifically. In fact, when SeaWorld animal care staff observed a Commerson's calf showing signs of exhaustion and possible malnutrition just sixteen days after birth, they knew just what to do. Find out more about this in the next chapter.

# Commerson's
# Care

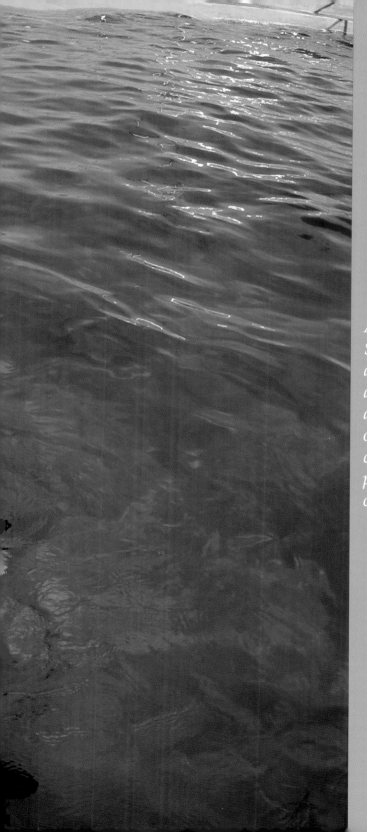

*An Animal Care
Specialist observes
and records each
animal's behavior
and appetite as part
of SeaWorld's
comprehensive
preventive medicine
care program.*

A dolphin presents its flipper for examination. Trained husbandry behaviors such as this are vital to evaluating animal health.

# Husbandry Training

Husbandry is the science and practice of caring for animals. SeaWorld bases its animal husbandry on a comprehensive preventive medicine program. Direct animal observation is the most useful diagnostic tool. Dolphins also are given regular physical exams. From this information veterinarians usually can detect health concerns early.

To assist with gathering vital health information, the dolphins are trained to present various parts of their bodies for examination, measurement, and blood sampling. They also are trained to hold still during exams, and some will even give a urine sample when signaled to do so. Trainers and veterinarians are able to perform delicate procedures, such as taking X-rays and obtaining sonogram data.

Training helps veterinarians, animal care specialists, and trainers gather information to form a complete picture of a dolphin's health and maintain detailed husbandry records. The information gained through these routine examinations is a valuable resource for the zoological community.

**A whistle is a common bridge signal used in dolphin training. A bridge signal lets the dolphin know it has succeeded.**

In the previous chapter, on page 37, you read about how animal care specialists observed a 16-day-old Commerson's dolphin calf that was showing signs of exhaustion and possible malnutrition. SeaWorld veterinarians determined that, although the calf was nursing, it was not receiving enough milk from its mother for normal growth and development.

## Baby Formula

| | |
|---|---|
| 562.5 g | herring fillets (heads, bones, fins, and skin removed) |
| 1.15 l | fresh water |
| 225 g | Zoologic® 33/40 milk matrix |
| 120 g | Zoologic® 30/55 milk matrix |
| 11.25 g | dextrose |
| 6.75 g | salt |
| 5.25 g | lecithin |
| 0.187 g | taurine (187 mg) |
| 3.75 | dicalcium phosphate tablets ground into powder |
| 37.5 ml | menhaden oil |
| 75 ml | heavy whipping cream |

(Zoologic® is a product of Pet-Ag, Inc. 201 Keyes Ave., Hampshire, IL, 60140)

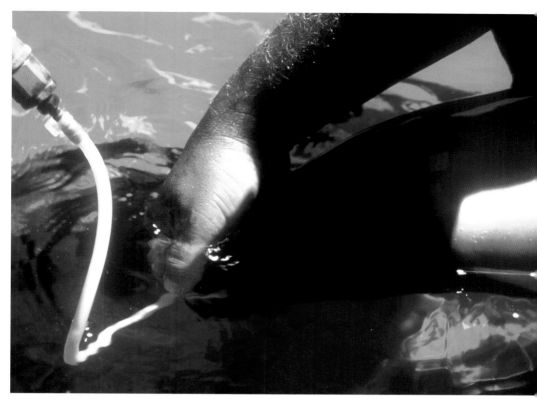

**This calf needed supplemental formula for normal weight gain and development. It received a specially developed formula by means of a tube.**

The calf was able to stay with its mother because animal care specialists supplemented about half of the dolphin calf's daily caloric needs with a special formula developed by SeaWorld veterinarians. The formula was full of vitamins, minerals, and plenty of calories for the growing calf. The calf was fed the thick formula through a tube.

After about two and a half months of both nursing and receiving the specially designed dolphin formula, the healthy calf was weaned from tube-feedings to eating small fishes. Besides feeding on fishes for most of its caloric requirements, the calf continued nursing from its mother until it was about 9 months old.

Not everyone has the chance to see these animals in the wild.

# Educational Value

Over the years, millions have visited marinelife parks such as SeaWorld to see dolphins and other animals. Kids of all ages participate in SeaWorld Adventure Camps.

Adventure Camps and other educational experiences at SeaWorld give guests an in-depth look at the characteristics, care, and conservation of aquatic animals.

The unique opportunity to observe and learn directly from live animals increases public awareness and appreciation of wildlife.

# Glossary

**bioacoustics** — the study of sounds produced or received by living organisms.

**blowhole** — the nostril at the top of the head in dolphins through which they breathe.

**blubber** — a layer of fat cells and fibrous connective tissue, between the skin and the muscle of most marine mammals.

**calf** — the young of certain large mammal species, such as whales, dolphins, and manatees.

**cetacean** — any of several large aquatic mammals that have forelimbs modified into flippers, a horizontally flattened tail, a nostril at the top of the head for breathing, and no hind limbs. Cetaceans include all whales, dolphins, and porpoises.

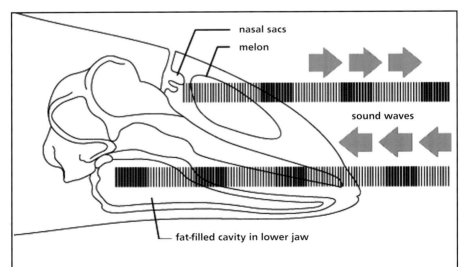

**Commerson's dolphins echolocate—they locate objects by emitting sound waves that pass through the melon, then receiving and interpreting the resulting echo. They receive sound through the fat-filled cavity in the lower jaw.**

**disruptive coloration** — color patterns that obscure the outline of an animal by contradicting the animal's body shape or by drawing attention to certain highly distinctive elements of the pattern.

**dorsal fin** — a fin on the back of a dolphin; a paddle-like appendage that helps the dolphin steer, swim, or maintain balance.

**echolocate** — to locate objects by emitting sound waves and interpreting the resulting echo.

**endangered** — in danger of becoming extinct.

**flipper** — a broad, flat limb supported by bones and modified for swimming.

**flukes** — the horizontal lobes of a dolphin's tail, made of connective tissue, not bone.

**gestation** — the period during which offspring are developing and carried within the mother's body.

**habitat** — the place where an animal lives.

**husbandry** — the science and practice of breeding and caring for animals.

**melon** — the rounded, fat-filled region of a dolphin's forehead.

**myoglobin** — an iron-containing protein in muscle tissue. Myoglobin transports and stores oxygen.

**piebald** — spotted or patched with black and white.

**rostrum** — a beaklike or snoutlike projection.

**thermoregulation** — processes by which an animal regulates body temperature.

**threatened** — likely to become endangered.

**trachea** — a tube inside an animal used for breathing. The trachea extends from the throat to the lungs.

# Web Sites

CITES <www.cites.org>

Convention on Migratory Species
<www.wcmc.org.uk/cms>

IUCN Redlist <www.redlist.org>

SeaWorld Animal Information <www.seaworld.org>

The Society for Marine Mammalogy
<www.marinemammalogy.org>

# Bibliography

Byrum, Jody. *A World Beneath the Waves. Whales, Dolphins, and Porpoises.* San Diego: SeaWorld Education Department Publications, 1998.

Minasian, Stanley M., Kenneth C. Balcomb, and Larry Foster. *The World's Whales.* Washington, D.C.: Smithsonian Books, 1984.

Cetacean Specialist Group. "*Cephalorhynchus commersonii.*" In *IUCN Red List of Threatened Species*, 1996. <www.redlist.org>

Culik, Boris M., ed. "*Cephalorhynchus commersonii* (Lacépède 1804)." In *Review On Small Cetaceans: Distribution, Behaviour, Migration, and Threats.* Compiled for the Convention on Migratory Species (CMS), 2003. <www.wcmc.org.uk/cms>

Goodall, R.N.P. "*Commerson's Dolphin* Cephalorhynchus commersonii *(Lacépède 1804).*" In S.H. Ridgway and R. Harrison (eds). *Handbook of Marine Mammals. Volume 5: The First Book of Dolphins*, pp. 241-267. London: Academic Press, 1994.

Kastelein, R.A., J. McBain, and B. Neurohr. "Information on the biology of Commerson's Dolphins (*Cephalorhynchus commersonii*)." In *Aquatic Mammals* 1993, 19.1, pp. 13–19.

Leatherwood, Stephen and Randall R. Reeves. *The Sierra Club Handbook of Whales and Dolphins*. San Francisco, California: Sierra Club Books, 1983.

Reeves, Randall R., Brent S. Stewart, Phillip J. Clapham, and James A. Powell. *Guide to Marine Mammals of the World*. New York: Alfred A. Knopf, 2002.

Perrin, William F, Bernd Würsig, and J.G.M. Thewissen, eds. *Encyclopedia of Marine Mammals*. San Diego, California: Academic Press, 2002.

## Books for Young Readers

Brust, Beth Wagner. *Zoobooks: Dolphins and Porpoises*. San Diego: Wildlife Education, Ltd., 1999.

Hatherly, Janelle and Delia Nicholls. *Dolphins and Porpoises. Great Creatures of the World*. New York: Facts On File, Inc., 1990.

Nuzzolo, Deborah. *This is a Dolphin*. San Diego: SeaWorld Books for Young Learners, 2002.

Parker, Steve. *Whales and Dolphins*. San Francisco: Sierra Club Books for Children, 1994.

Reeves, Randall R. and Stephen Leatherwood. *The Sea World Book of Dolphins*. San Diego: Harcourt Brace Jovanovich, Publishers, 1987.

Rinard, Judith E. *Dolphins. Our Friends in the Sea. Dolphins and Other Toothed Whales*. Washington D.C.: The National Geographic Society, 1986.

# Index

# Goals of the SeaWorld and Busch Gardens Education Departments

Based on a long-term commitment to education, SeaWorld and Busch Gardens strive to provide an enthusiastic, imaginative, and intellectually stimulating atmosphere to help students and guests develop a lifelong appreciation, understanding, and stewardship for our environment. Specifically, our goals are...

- To instill in students and guests of all ages an appreciation for science and a respect for all living creatures and habitats.
- To conserve our valuable natural resources by increasing awareness of the interrelationships of humans and the environment.
- To increase students' and guests' basic competencies in science, math, and other disciplines.
- To be an educational resource to the world.

*"For in the end we will conserve only what we love. We will love only what we understand. We will understand only what we are taught." — B. Dioum*

## Want more information?

Visit the SeaWorld/Busch Gardens Animal Information Database at *www.seaworld.org* or *www.buschgardens.org*

Still have questions? E-mail: *shamu@seaworld.org* or call 1-800-23-SHAMU (1-800-237-4268). TDD users call 1-800-TD-SHAMU (1-800-837-4268). Emails and phones are answered by SeaWorld Educators.

SeaWorld has books, teacher's guides, posters, and videos available on a variety of animals and topics. Call 1-800-23SHAMU to request an Educational Materials catalog or shop online at *swbg-estore.com*

## Anheuser-Busch Adventure Parks

| | | |
|---|---|---|
| **SeaWorld Orlando** | **SeaWorld San Antonio** | **SeaWorld San Diego** |
| (800) 406-2244 | (210) 523-3608 | (800) 237-4268 |
| 7007 Sea World Drive | 10500 Sea World Drive | 500 Sea World Drive |
| Orlando, FL 32821-8097 | San Antonio, TX 78251-3002 | San Diego, CA 92109-7904 |
| | | |
| **Discovery Cove** | **Busch Gardens Tampa Bay** | **Busch Gardens Williamsburg** |
| (877) 434-7268 | (813) 987-5555 | (800) 343-7946 |
| 6000 Discovery Cove Way | 3605 E. Bougainvillea Ave. | One Busch Gardens Blvd. |
| Orlando, FL 32821-8097 | Tampa, FL 33612 | Williamsburg, VA 23187-8785 |